How Our Children
Come to Faith

Basics of the Faith

How Do We Glorify God?
How Our Children Come to Faith
What Are Election and Predestination?
What Is a Reformed Church?
What Is a True Calvinist?
What Is Biblical Preaching?
What Is Church Government?
What Is Hell?
What Is Justification by Faith Alone?
What Is Perseverance of the Saints?
What Is Providence?
What Is Spiritual Warfare?
What Is the Christian Worldview?
What Is the Lord's Supper?
What Is True Conversion?
What Is Vocation?
What Is Worship Music?
Why Do We Baptize Infants?

How Our
Children
Come to Faith

Stephen E. Smallman

P&R
PUBLISHING
P.O. BOX 817 • PHILLIPSBURG • NEW JERSEY 08865-0817

Page design by Tobias Design

Printed in the United States of America

Library of Congress Control Number: 2006934625

ISBN-13: 978-1-59638-053-0

INTRODUCTION

I still remember the birth of my firstborn as though it were yesterday. Like any other new parents, Sandy and I were overwhelmed with a mixture of joy and responsibility. But as Christian parents, we also had a sense that this child had been given to us by God, and it was our longing and prayer that our son would one day trust his eternal soul to Jesus Christ as Lord and Savior, just as we had done. I was a fairly new believer with no church background and had never studied theology or church tradition. But I knew that I wanted to publicly give my child to God. I also desired prayer that Sandy and I would be godly parents. I had not completed my education, and we were spending the summer with my mother-in-law. The pastor of the church we were attending welcomed our request, and we dedicated ourselves and our baby to Christ on a Sunday morning before we returned to school.

I continued my studies as well as my personal spiritual pilgrimage, and by the time our second child was born, I was persuaded that baptism was the biblical means of setting apart our children for God. We brought both of our children for baptism in the Presbyterian church we had recently joined. In the years that followed, the Lord gave us two more children, whom we also presented for baptism. I say, with gratitude to God, that all four of our children are actively serving Christ along with their Christian spouses. We give God glory for his faithfulness to two young and inexperienced parents.

I'm writing this as a father and grandfather as well as a pastor for over forty years, and I'm glad to contribute to this series of booklets by P&R Publishing called Basics of the Faith. The matter of passing along the faith to our children is certainly one of those basics. One of the things that initially attracted me to the Presbyterian church was its emphasis on thinking in terms of generations rather than just personal faith. I'm writing to parents in a Presbyterian or other Reformed church setting, but I hope this booklet will be helpful to other Christian parents as well. These are truths I wish I had understood as I began the exciting and yet awesome pilgrimage of raising children.

The heart of the matter is that we parents want to instill in our children the desire to follow Jesus, but we are also profoundly aware that we are inadequate to the task. And we are! Therefore, we come to God and ask for his help—which is the very best thing we can do. But in my pastoral experience, too many Christian parents are so focused on their responsibility for their children's spiritual lives that their prayers are essentially, "Lord, help me do *my* job and fulfill *my* calling to raise my children in the faith." They don't stop and listen *first* to what God has told them about *his* commitment to our children. I want to help the parent, grandparent, caregiver, or teacher of children to do this. The realization that our children's salvation is in God's hands is not meant to take away the role that God has given us. Nevertheless, the foundation for what we do for our children is to understand and believe

what God has said about his work for them and in them. As
with any other aspect of the Christian life, raising our children in the Lord then becomes what the apostle Paul called
"the obedience that comes from faith" (Rom. 1:5).

I am not writing to teach about the baptism of our children. I came to that position from a biblical and theological
perspective, and my conviction of its validity has strength-
ened through the years. Nevertheless, the inward conviction
by parents that our children are gifts *from* God and *for* God is
not limited to those who practice infant baptism. For those
who want to pursue this question further, there are some ex-
cellent resources from P&R Publishing.[1] I am also not ad-
dressing difficult questions such as the death of children or
children who turn away from the faith of their parents.[2] These
are very important, but the purpose of this booklet is to try to
explain the usual way in which God works to bring our children to faith.

Furthermore, this is not a booklet about the "how to" of
parenting or spiritual nurture. Without question, these sub-
jects are very important and deserve far more attention than I
can give in this brief essay. Ample books, seminars, etc., are
available to encourage and support Christian parents. Most of
what is written and taught is helpful as long as we remember
that "surefire" methodologies don't always work. We parents
are sinners who have our own struggles and will never be able
to "get it right" when it comes to raising children. I have often
said that Peter's word, "Love covers over a multitude of sins"
(1 Peter 4:8), was my salvation as a parent. We tried to make
sure that our children were told and shown that they were
deeply and unconditionally loved, but beyond that I can't hold
up any great secret to raising Christian children.

As a pastor, I have frequently had calls from people I didn't know asking if I would baptize their baby. Even though they weren't members of the church, I invited them to come and talk, explaining that when we baptized a child it also meant that we received them as members of the church and pledged to support the parents in the spiritual nurture of their child. Baptism would be only an empty ceremony without the commitments that go with it. Therefore, we needed to talk first about the parents' commitment to Christ and the church. Most of the time I was given a polite "thank you" and never heard from them again. But on several occasions that call was the starting point of a new walk with Christ. Perhaps you are reading this as a parent who wants to begin providing a spiritual dimension for your family. Even though you have not been actively serving Christ up to this point, God has given you a child, and you know that you need to rethink your priorities now that you are a parent. As you read this booklet to learn about how your children come to faith, consider also what it means for you yourself to be a believer.

BRINGING OUR CHILDREN TO JESUS

Throughout this booklet I refer to "our" children. That is very deliberate. When I speak of "how *our* children come to faith," I am speaking about the children of people who profess to be followers of Jesus. We are those who are sincerely looking to Jesus for our own salvation as well as that of our children. Therefore, the best starting point for considering how those children come to faith is to look to Jesus himself.

Begin by thoughtfully reading and considering this incident recorded in the gospel according to Matthew:

Then little children were brought to Jesus for him to place his hands on them and pray for them. But the disciples rebuked those who brought them. Jesus said, "Let the little children come to me, and do not hinder them, for the kingdom of heaven belongs to such as these." When he had placed his hands on them, he went on from there. (Matt. 19:13–15)

There were times when Jesus used children to illustrate childlike faith (Matt. 18:2–6; Mark 10:13–16; Luke 18:15–17). But in this incident recorded in Matthew 19, it is clear that Jesus is actually speaking about little children. These are children who were brought to Jesus by parents or others who loved them and who desired that Jesus would bless them by placing his hand on them. Jesus was upset that the disciples tried to discourage the parents ("indignant" is the word used by Mark). The disciples were probably thinking that the Messiah had far more important things to do than pay attention to children. But Jesus makes an emphatic statement that these parents were doing the right thing. He said, "Let the little children come to me," and just in case they missed the point he added, "and do not hinder them." He then reached out and placed his hand of blessing on their heads. Mark records that he held them in his arms as he did this.

We could view this simply as a beautiful picture of Jesus loving little children, but a statement from him gives this incident far more significance. As he rebuked the disciples and blessed the children, he added: "for the kingdom of heaven belongs to such as these." *He opened his kingdom to little children.* The way in which Jesus said this leaves room for various interpretations, but at the very least it is clear that Jesus was welcoming little children who were brought to him. The great Reformer John Calvin, commenting on this verse, said, "It is an irreligious audacity to drive from Christ's fold those whom He nursed in his bosom, and to shut the door on them as strangers when He did not wish to forbid them."[3]

The children in the gospel passage received that blessed touch of Jesus because it is what the parents wanted for their children and they took necessary measures to make it happen. They were determined even when the disciples mistakenly tried to turn them away. It was not the children who exercised faith; it was those bringing them to Jesus. No doubt the children were of various ages, but the account in Luke makes it clear that they included infants (Luke 18:15). Several other passages in the gospel records tell of Jesus' honoring the faith of parents by blessing or healing their children.[4]

When we begin to consider our part in our children's coming to faith, this is the first thing we are to do—*we bring them to Jesus*. When we hear Jesus say that "the kingdom of heaven belongs to such as these," we hold our children before him and say, "Yes, Lord, I believe that promise, and I claim it for my child." This duty begins as personal prayers of the parents, but bringing our children to Jesus also needs some kind of public expression. Historically, that expression has been made through baptism, but even in churches that do not practice the baptism of children, some means have been found to give parents the opportunity to publicly bring them to Jesus for blessing and dedication.

In fact, bringing our children into the assembly of God's people for a blessing *is* to bring them into the presence of

Jesus. He is now the risen and ascended Christ who also dwells with his people when they gather. The church is called the body of Christ, and Jesus himself assured us of his presence when even two or three gather in his name (Matt. 18:20). Vern Poythress beautifully expresses this truth:

> When we translate this picture into the present time, it becomes if anything even more profound. Parents bring their children to Jesus in Christian worship. And what does Jesus do? Jesus receives them! He embraces them. He is the divine mediator, with all authority in heaven and on earth, who opens the way into the Most Holy Place, the throne-room of God. In priestly prayer, as the final intercessor before God, he blesses them with the blessings of God.[5]

I Will Be Your God and the God of Your Children

What Jesus was demonstrating in his readiness to bless the children is fully consistent with what is revealed throughout Scripture about the character of God and his promises. One of the characteristics of God as he is revealed in the Bible is that he constantly enters into covenants with his people. God Almighty actually commits himself to be faithful and loyal to a people who are always going their own way. When God makes a covenant, he typically speaks of that covenant's being passed along to the coming generations. For example, he said to Abraham:

> I will establish my covenant as an everlasting covenant between me and you *and your descendants*

after you for the generations to come, to be your God and the God *of your descendants* after you. (Gen. 17:7)

Read the first eleven chapters of Deuteronomy. These are sermons that Moses preached to the Israelites just before they entered the Promised Land. While there are many warnings and calls for obedience, these Scriptures teach that entering the land was a fulfillment of a covenant God had made with their fathers, which he was fulfilling for the Israelites and would fulfill for generations to come. In other words, it is the nature of God to make and keep covenants, and the people could count on this for future generations.

It was because the LORD loved you and kept the oath he swore to your forefathers that he brought you out with a mighty hand and redeemed you from the land of slavery, from the power of Pharaoh king of Egypt. Know therefore that the LORD your God is God; he is the faithful God, keeping his covenant of love to a thousand generations of those who love him and keep his commands. (Deut. 7:8–9)

I myself had a personal encounter with this great truth, and I am seeing it lived out in a third generation. Several months before I was married (and years before I became a Presbyterian), I was reading in Isaiah and came across this verse:

As for me, *this is my covenant* with them, saith the LORD; My spirit that is upon thee, and my words which I have put in thy mouth, shall not depart out of thy mouth, *nor out of the mouth of thy seed, nor out of the mouth of thy seed's seed*, saith the LORD, from henceforth and for ever. (Isa. 59:21 KJV)

In the margin of the Bible I was reading, I wrote, "For Our Family," and added a date: "2/4/60." That was over a year before our wedding and more than two years before our first child was born, but I claimed that promise for the children and grandchildren that had not yet been born. I laid that Bible aside for years as I read other versions. When I was preparing to participate in the baptism of my first grandchild, I was drawn to pick up my old Bible and to look at this verse. I rediscovered my little note and the date, and I was overwhelmed with thanksgiving to realize that I was about to mark a very literal fulfillment of God's promise claimed thirty years earlier. Through tears of joy I said to the little gathering of believers, "God has kept his promise." As of this writing, that grandson has publicly confessed his faith in Jesus and is following the God of his parents and grandparents.

You Will Be Saved and Your Household

There may still be a question about just how this wonderful truth of God's covenant-making and covenant-keeping applies to our situation. After all, we are no longer a nation inhabiting a land. Isn't the setting of the New Testament different? Yes, the setting is different, but the promises of God are still true.

On the day of Pentecost when the gift of the Holy Spirit was given to the church, Peter immediately assured his hearers that this "promise is for you *and your children*" (Acts 2:39). That was a gathering of Jewish people whose culture was rooted in the understanding that children were part of the spiritual community. The physical sign of that community was the circumcision of male children. Peter made a point of assuring them that in this new age that had just come, that understanding would still be true.

But this assurance is also reflected in the way the gospel was proclaimed to the Gentiles. Paul told the jailer in Philippi, "Believe in the Lord Jesus, and you will be saved— you *and your household*," and later that evening that man "and all his family were baptized" (Acts 16:31–33). Earlier in that same chapter, the Scripture records that a woman named Lydia was listening to Paul preach the gospel and "the Lord opened her heart to respond to Paul's message," following which "she *and the members of her household* were baptized" (Acts 16:14–15). Paul writing to the Corinthian church told believing spouses not to leave their unbelieving partners and then referred to their children as "holy" (1 Cor. 7:14) because they were part of a home with even one believing parent.

In the light of the clear revelation of the Old and New Testaments, we are right to conclude that it is the character of God to pass his salvation from generation to generation, and this is still true. In fact, the promise in Isaiah 59 that meant so much to me turns out to be more than an Old Testament promise. When examined in the context of surrounding chapters, it is actually a prophecy of what is called the *new* covenant. This is the covenant that came with Jesus and is to be proclaimed to all the nations.

When we pray for our children and work with them in our homes and churches, God's covenant-making and covenant-keeping should give us confidence that it is his purpose and plan to pass his salvation from generation to generation. In the Presbyterian tradition, we use the expression *covenant children*[6] to describe their unique standing before God. That is a very helpful and biblical way to think of our children. *Having this confidence in God's faithfulness to his covenant promises is the most important single thing we can do for the salvation of our children.* We should pray for them with earnestness, but pray with confidence because God has clearly revealed his will for our children *and he keeps his promises.* Those of you reading this whose children are older, and who have seemingly turned away from the faith or have become indifferent, should continue to pray earnestly for them, based on the promises of God. Pray boldly, like the persistent widow before the judge (Luke 18:1–8). This does not in any way diminish our responsibility for their spiritual nurture; in fact, I think it frees us to do a more effective job.

SUMMARY AND THOUGHTS FOR DISCUSSION OR REFLECTION

- What is your spiritual heritage? Were you blessed to "inherit" faith from godly parents, or are you beginning a new line of believers?
- Are you a parent whose sense of responsibility has kept you from first appreciating what the Lord has said about his commitments to your children?
- Give some thought to the picture of Jesus holding little children in his arms and blessing them. Have you thought about the baptism of your children in that light?
- Do you appreciate how the covenantal nature of God's dealing with us is as valid for us in our day as it was for the Old Testament believers?

YOU MUST BE BORN AGAIN

We began consideration of the salvation of our children by hearing the words of Jesus. Now hear another word from him that speaks not specifically of children but of anyone who would enter the kingdom of God. Jesus said, "I tell you the truth, unless a man is born again, he cannot see the kingdom of God" (John 3:3). A study of the full passage (3:1–8) makes it clear that Jesus is describing a supernatural work of the Holy Spirit in the human spirit by using the familiar imagery of birth. "Flesh gives birth to flesh, but the Spirit gives birth to spirit" (3:6).

In a great deal of popular teaching, being born again is viewed as something that people themselves make happen by "accepting Jesus as personal Savior" or other terms that speak of believing or making a decision. But this is *not* what Jesus is describing in the passage. This is a work that only God can do, an inward transformation that is like a birth. We were certainly present for our first birth, but we didn't make it happen; and that is equally true for our spiritual birth. So when Jesus said we "must" be born again (3:7), it was not a command, but a statement of what the Spirit must do before a person can enter the kingdom of God. In theological language this is *regeneration*, whereas the choice to believe in Jesus is part of *conversion*. *It is vital to understand that these are different.* Regeneration is described in John 3:1–8 and conversion in 3:14–18. Regeneration is the mysterious, supernatural work of the Spirit ("The wind blows wherever it pleases. . . . So it is with everyone born of the Spirit," 3:8), and conversion is the human response to that supernatural work ("whoever believes in him shall not perish but have eternal life," 3:16).

The traditional statement of the Reformed tradition is that "regeneration precedes faith." In other words, personal salvation is possible because God opens our hearts and enables us to believe.[7] The distinction between regeneration and conversion is essential if we are to understand how our children come to faith. In the first place, the question of whether they need to be born again is very clearly answered by Jesus. They must be born again—there is no other way to enter the kingdom. While our children are blessed to be born in a covenant relationship with God, they are also part of the fallen race that is dead in trespass and sin, and are "*by nature* objects of wrath."[8] Notice that the text says it is our nature, rather than our actions or thoughts, that places us under the wrath of God. This means that our children's inclination to sin (like ours) is part of who they *are*, not just what they *do*. I have often commented that "original sin" is not a doctrine that we need to prove from Scripture (although it is certainly biblical)—we just have to spend some time with children! Our little "angels" demonstrate very quickly that they are sinners in need of regeneration. But once we understand that regeneration is a hidden work of God, then we can pray and believe that the Spirit would begin that work very early in our children's lives. It will probably be several years before our children express that faith in a public confession. But that doesn't mean the Spirit hasn't been at work from a very early point in their lives. I think many parents are particularly zealous to press their children to make some sort of "decision for Jesus" because they think that such a point marks the beginning of their spiritual lives. Actually, the beginning is the mysterious work that only the Spirit can do.

For most of the Christian church throughout its history, the prayer of Christian parents that God would regenerate their children has been linked to baptism. In fact, many traditions quote John 3:5 ("unless a man is born of water and the Spirit") to teach that baptism *is* the new birth. This doctrine is called *baptismal regeneration*. It is taught that the water of baptism is necessary for the Spirit to work in regeneration. This is what is behind the call for clergymen to baptize miscarried unborn children or dying babies. Churches of the Reformed tradition do not insist on this because they teach that children should be baptized because they are *already* "holy in Christ," not that baptism makes them holy.

If you are not part of a tradition that baptizes children, you can at least respect the sincere conviction that lies behind that practice. It is true, unfortunately, that baptism is misused. In too many instances, the water of baptism is given virtually magical powers to transform a child. For others, the baptism of children is little more than a family celebration. But there are also many, many examples of parents' bringing their children to Christ as an act of faith to ask for his blessing on them. As they see the water applied outwardly, they trust that the Spirit will also be at work inwardly. It is God who will save our children, not baptism, and we can pray that he will start that work in their hearts early in their lives.

Here is a beautiful expression of that idea written in 1844 by Archibald Alexander, a pastor and founding professor of Princeton Theological Seminary:

> If piety may commence at any age, how solicitous should parents be for their children, that God would

bestow His grace upon them, even before they know their right hand from their left; and, when about to dedicate them to God in holy baptism, how earnestly should they pray that they might be baptized with the Holy Ghost—that while their bodies are washed in the emblematic laver of regeneration, their souls may experience the renewing of the Holy Ghost, and the sprinkling of the blood of Jesus. If such sentiments expressed above be correct, then may there be such a thing as baptismal regeneration; not that the mere external application of water can have any effect to purify the soul; nor that internal grace uniformly or generally accompanies this external washing, but that God, who works when and by what means He pleases, may regenerate by His Spirit the soul of the infant, while in His sacred name, water is applied to the body.[9]

SUMMARY AND THOUGHTS FOR DISCUSSION OR REFLECTION

· Make sure that you stop and consider the distinction between regeneration and conversion. Do you understand how it is possible to think of the Spirit at work in little children, even though they are not yet believers?

· Do you have a new appreciation of the importance of baptism? Do you have some prejudices you need to overcome based on the abuses of the sacrament you have seen?

THE CONVERSION OF OUR CHILDREN

When the Holy Spirit works in the inward spiritual transformation called regeneration, the result is a person who comes to trust in Jesus Christ alone for salvation. As I mentioned earlier, this can be called *conversion*. It is a turning away from focus on self and sin (repentance) to a trust in Jesus as Lord and Savior (faith). In the case of the classic conversion story we often hear, a person begins in a condition of unbelief. The people who were reached in the New Testament were in that condition. They had never heard of the name of Jesus, whether they were Jews or Gentiles. Conversion to Christ meant a deliberate step away from the old way to following a new way. This is what we could call a "first generation" conversion, and of course, it is still going on today. Many of you reading this booklet came to faith in Christ from an unbelieving background. You have a clear memory of your conversion, whether it was a dramatic experience or a season of life during which you came to a knowledge of Christ for the first time.

Conversion, however, is not always such a clear step for our children. Consider the fact that our children are being raised in a very different situation. They are part of a family that is *already* on the path of following Christ. Coming to Christ for them does not mean turning from and renouncing an unbelieving life. They have been raised to believe in Jesus—that is what you have been praying for from the very beginning.

The question should then be asked: Do our children need to be converted? The answer to that is *yes*, as long as we don't define *conversion* in terms of a particular kind of experience. In a companion booklet in this series, I have defined *conversion* in the words of the Westminster Shorter Catechism as "embracing Jesus Christ, freely offered to us in the gospel."[10] Based on this definition, our children most certainly need to be converted—but that conversion could be so much a part of their lives that they grow up never knowing a time when they weren't embracing Jesus Christ freely offered in the gospel.

In another example of Jesus' referring to children, he said, "Unless you change and become like little children, you will never enter the kingdom of heaven" (Matt. 18:3). The word *change* means literally, "turn" or "turn around," which is the essential idea of conversion. If Jesus used children and their simple trust to illustrate entering the kingdom, then we can assume that children can exercise such faith.

There is no one way to describe how our children will experience conversion. Some will always believe, even though they may go through seasons of doubt. Other children will struggle to believe and have a specific memory of a conversion. I have spoken to many raised in solid Christian homes who remember an early experience of conversion but who walked away from it until many years later. Others never knew a time they didn't believe and never seriously wandered from that path.

The matter of how to make sure that our children are "saved" is a source of real anxiety for many conscientious Christian parents. Concerned parents begin to "evangelize" their children as soon as they are able to talk. They load up on books and videos, Bible lessons, Scripture memory, etc., trying to make sure that the children are saturated with godly influences. Then they proudly announce that Mary, at age three or four, has "received Christ as her Lord" because she prayed some variation of the sinner's prayer or answered the call at a vacation Bible school or Sunday school meeting. Loving teachers or youth leaders ask our children over and over whether they are "really sure" they have accepted Jesus. After a while they *aren't* sure—because they don't know which time they prayed the prayer was the "real" time. One of my children tells about making up a "testimony" to finally satisfy his youth leaders that he was a believer.

That is all well-intentioned, but I wonder if it is the best approach. How much of this way of dealing with children is a consequence of feeling that their salvation hangs on how effective we are in evangelizing them? I want to encourage you instead to start with an awareness of God's wonderful promises and to rest in those promises. Of course we have great responsibilities, but that can't be our starting place.

If we build on the foundation of God's promises and Jesus' statement about our children, then we can view the salvation of our children from the perspective of *faith* rather than *anxiety*. And by faith, we then set about the privilege of raising our children "in the training and instruction of the Lord" (Eph. 6:4). The word that better fits this admonition is *discipleship* rather than *evangelism*. The earliest disciples were following Jesus even while they were learning what it meant to believe in him. Can't it be said that our children are part of a family of Jesus' disciples and that in that sense, they themselves are also disciples? As the family serves the Lord, led by the head of the household, the members of the family learn together what it means to embrace Jesus personally. A simple example of this form of discipleship is teaching our children to pray the Lord's Prayer. When we teach them to say, "Our Father," that is true for them because the God and Father of Jesus is also the God and Father of our family, even if our children do not yet comprehend what it means to believe in him.

The term used in earlier generations to describe this more discipleship-oriented way of passing along the faith was *Christian nurture*. The question of how children come to faith received a great deal of attention in the Presbyterian church with the rise of revivalism in the nineteenth century. So much attention was given to dramatic conversion stories that the "boring" examples of people growing up and receiving the faith passed along to them by their families were considered invalid. In some ways it became a self-fulfilling prophecy. Because such ordinary means as family prayers, catechizing children, and faithful church attendance were being set aside to wait for the next great season of revival, many children were leaving the faith of their fathers. I remember hearing the catchy phrase that came out of that era, "God has no grandchildren," and finding it appealing because it described my situation. In one sense it is true that God doesn't have grandchildren, but if that means every person, including those raised in Christian homes, come into the world as pagans with no relationship to God, then it is not true. Lewis Bevens Schenck did a helpful (and very academic) study of this controversy and concluded: "Christian nurture was, then, the appointed, the natural, the normal, and ordinary means by which the children of believers were made truly the children of God. Consequently it was the method which these leaders believed should be principally relied upon and employed for the salvation of their children."[11]

A Profession of Faith and Communion

Many of us who have been strongly influenced by the evangelical culture of recent decades have looked at the personal experience of "accepting Jesus" as the defining spiritual moment. In fact, traditionally, and I believe biblically, the more important moment is the time of public confession of Christ. In the case of those coming as unbelievers and converted as adults, this is the time of baptism and admission to the Lord's Supper. The New Testament was written in a setting where everyone was coming into the church in this way. The few actual examples recorded in the New Testament indicate that they came in as family units as well as individually. But there is no description of how those children were to enter into the full communion of the church as they grew older and in turn married and raised children who were already in the community of believers. Church historians have not been able to identify exactly what was practiced in the early church.[12]

Not surprisingly, then, there has been any number of practices with reference to the public profession of children from Christian families. Even within the Presbyterian tradition that I am part of, I have observed quite a few different approaches to this important matter. Rather than prescribe yet another approach to this question, I would simply encourage parents and church leaders to recognize what a fundamentally important step it is. Every culture has some form of "coming-of-age" ceremony. This seems to be part of God's pattern for social interaction, and it should be part of the way in which the Christian community functions.

To be sure, only God can see whether a heart is truly regenerate, which is true of adults as well as children. But from a human perspective, the primary evidence of a regenerate heart is a readiness to "confess with your mouth, 'Jesus is Lord' " (Rom. 10:9; see also 1 Cor. 12:3). The Romans passage goes on to state: "For it is with your heart that you believe and are justified, and *it is with your mouth that you confess and are saved*" (Rom. 10:10). Churches that consider the discipleship of their children to be a primary responsibility must provide the means to equip children to make this confession of Christ with sincerity and understanding.[13] Typically, this is described as "joining the church." But for children raised in Christian homes, who are already part of the church, this step is not joining as much as publicly affirming that they are following the path of their parents.

Those who publicly confess Christ are welcome to join in the Lord's Supper. In churches I have pastored, I made it a practice to receive new members on a communion Sunday. This is particularly important when children and young people are being welcomed. Those who were not baptized as infants are baptized on profession of faith, and then all are invited to join with the church in participating in the highest privilege a church can give—communion in the body and blood of her Lord.

The point at which our children publicly confess Christ and begin to take communion is not the end of our discipleship by any means. But this is a time when we should stop and reflect on the faithfulness of God. We who have been blessed to hear and believe the gospel can rejoice to say that we have seen that faith passed to another generation. He is a God who keeps his promises.

SUMMARY AND THOUGHTS FOR DISCUSSION OR REFLECTION

· Reflect on your own coming to faith. What were the earliest ways in which you began to awaken to Christ? Did you have a dramatic conversion? Try to talk to another believer whose experience was quite different from yours to realize the various ways that God works in the heart.

· If you did not grow up in a good church and Christian home, try to talk to some who did to learn about their "conversions." How has this study affected your thinking about the conversion of children?

· Give some more attention to the old idea of Christian nurture. Do you understand the point that this should be the ordinary way in which our children come to faith?

· Do you know how your church prepares children to make a public profession of faith? Do you think it is satisfactory?

· If you are a pastor or leader in your church, are you like the disciples who were rebuked for their indifference to the need for parents to bring their children to Jesus? What can be done to support families and work as a team in the spiritual nurture of their children?

NOTES

1 For example, a very helpful booklet is John P. Sartelle's *What Christian Parents Should Know about Infant Baptism* (Phillipsburg, NJ: Presbyterian and Reformed Publishing, 1985) and Bryan Chapell's *Why Do We Baptize Infants?* (Phillipsburg, NJ: P&R Publishing, 2007).

2 See Timothy A. Sisemore, *Of Such Is the Kingdom* (Ross-shire, UK: Christian Focus, 2000). This is a biblical and practical book about the nature of children and how they should be nurtured at home and church. It deals very well with several difficult questions.

3 John Calvin, *Calvin's New Testament Commentaries*, vol. 2, *A Harmony of the Gospels* (Grand Rapids: Eerdmans, 1972), 252.

4 Mark 5:22–24, 35–43; 7:24–30.

5 Vern Poythress, "Linking Small Children with Infants in the Theology of Baptizing," *Westminster Theological Journal* 59 (1997): 148–49.

6 A recent volume deliberately emphasizes calling infant baptism "covenantal baptism" to make the point that the covenant is of the essence of the ceremony. See Gregg Strawbridge, ed., *The Case for Covenantal Infant Baptism* (Phillipsburg, NJ: P&R Publishing, 2003).

7 See my other writing on this important issue, *What Is True Conversion?* (Phillipsburg, NJ: P&R, Publishing, 2005) and *Spiritual Birthline: Understanding How We Experience the New Birth* (Wheaton, IL: Crossway Books, 2006).

8 Ephesians 2:1–3. In the full passage (2:1–10), Paul uses the imagery of resurrection instead of birth, but it is another way of picturing regeneration. We are dead in our sin, but God, who is rich in mercy, makes us alive in Christ.

9 Archibald Alexander, *Thoughts on Religious Experience* (Edinburgh: Banner of Truth Trust, 1967), 13. Originally published in 1844.

10 Westminster Shorter Catechism, answer to question 31; see also Smallman, *What Is True Conversion?*, 18–19.

11 Lewis Bevens Schenck, *The Presbyterian Doctrine of Children in the Covenant* (Phillipsburg, NJ: P&R Publishing, 2003), 145. Schenck includes a very helpful discussion of the confusing idea of presumptive regeneration (pp. 13off.).

12 Peter J. Leithart argues that even when infant baptism was clearly established as the practice of the church, the concept of covenantal baptism had been lost, in favor of the sacerdotal understanding. "Infant Baptism in History: An Unfinished Tragicomedy," chap. 12 in Strawbridge, *The Case for Covenantal Infant Baptism*.

13 As a possible resource, you may wish to consider *Understanding the Faith*, a workbook I have prepared for those making a profession of faith. Stephen Smallman, *Understanding the Faith* (Phillipsburg, NJ: P&R Publishing, 2001).

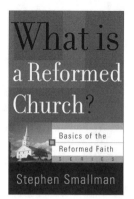

Also in the **Basics of the Faith** Series

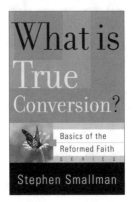

Price: $3.99
To order, visit www.prpbooks.com
or call 1(800) 631-0094

With his personal and warm style, Stephen Smallman explains the roles of the Father, the Son, and the Spirit in conversion. The review questions at the end of each section allow you to stop and apply the material to your own experience.

"This little booklet could help solve one of the greatest problems in churches today—confusion over what it means to really become a Christian. With the sure touch of a humble Christian and a faithful pastor, Steve Smallman has served us well by giving a brief and biblical treatment of conversion."

—MARK DEVER

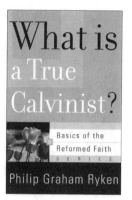

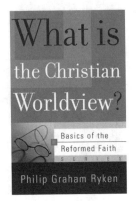
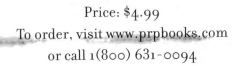